TISSUE P

Dere

Tissue Paper Magic

TISSUE PAPER MAGIC

Anyone can make beautiful pictures using bleeding tissue paper. Examples and projects are included along with strategies and techniques to build confidence.

Bleeding art tissue paper can be purchased at your favorite art supply store. However, to ensure you have the correct materials to be successful, please plan on ordering some supplies online. Recommendations for specific products and supplies are included. A budget of $20 will go a long way with this hobby.

The book begins with basic concepts and includes plenty of ideas that can be adapted for younger artists. Artists younger than 12 would require direction from a parent or older student. Some material near the end of the book should be considered advanced.

I am happy to share this fun and easy method to create beautiful pictures and thank you for sharing your time with me!

TYPES OF TISSUE PAPER

Tissue paper is manufactured in a variety of sizes, colors and types. And tissue paper can be used for many purposes.

If you were using the paper to wrap a gift, you might choose a color-fast tissue paper. Color-fast tissue paper uses color that will not bleed from the paper when wet.

Bleeding art tissue paper is a special type of tissue paper that releases its colors, and magic, when it becomes wet.

You will find bleeding tissue offered from a variety of manufacturers and vendors. The strategies and techniques discussed in this book will work with any brand, but will produce unique and different results.

All of the pictures and projects contained in this book are made using Spectra Art Tissue.

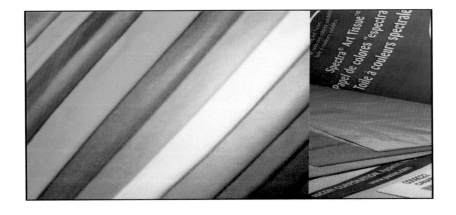

SPECTRA BLEEDING ART TISSUE

This beautiful tissue paper is available in 24 colors! Sold in packages of 20 sheets, each sheet measure 20 x 30 inches.

If you want to find out if this is a good hobby for you, start with the 24-color assortment of Spectra Art Tissue. You will have samples of all the colors, and enough paper to make many beautiful projects.

(5) **Blues**: Sky Blue, Azure Blue, French Blue, Medium Blue, and National Blue

(3) **Greens**: Spring Green, Apple Green, and Emerald

(3) **Purples**: Orchid, Purple, and Pansy

(7) **Reds and Pinks**: Blush Pink, Dark Pink, Cerise, Magenta, Scarlet, Chinese Red, and National Red

(3) **Yellow and Orange**: Canary Yellow, Goldenrod, and Orange

(3) **Neutral Colors**: Black, White, and Seal Brown

TYPES OF PAPERS AND BOARDS

Choosing the right paper surface to use with bleeding art tissue is the most important consideration. Bleeding tissue paper produces spectacular effects, but requires a suitable paper product for the ink to transfer properly

Every type of paper, poster board, or illustration board is going to behave differently when you apply tissue paper ink. Several factors, including the absorbability of the paper, will determine how well the ink from the tissue paper can be transferred.

Superior results can be achieved from paper that contains rag content or cotton fibers. This is the reason some poster board will work well, but office paper would not be a good choice.

There are four main types of paper products that you may want to consider.

1. Crescent Illustration Board
2. Strathmore Bristol Board
3. Poster board
4. Other Special Papers including cardstock watercolor Paper

The majority of the projects made in this book were made using Crescent Illustration Board. I have also included some examples which use Strathmore Bristol Board and poster board.

POSTER BOARD

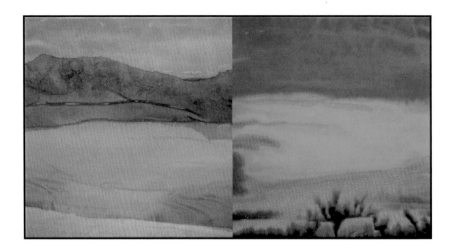

Poster board is often the most inexpensive and easily accessible material to use and can be a great medium to use with the bleeding tissue paper.

The number of layers and quality of the product will affect how well the ink is received. You will encounter noticeable differences between every brand and manufacturer. If you are fortunate, you may find poster board that works perfectly for the projects that you want to make.

STRATHMORE BRISTOL PAPER

This paper is a pleasure to work with and is available in different types and thicknesses. Offered in Velum and Plate. (Cold Press and Hot Press respectively). Professional artists may want to consider the 500 Series.

The 4 PLY BRISTOL PAPER is available in both regular and smooth finish. If you can only choose one, try the regular finish, though both fun to work with.

The sheet size is 22 x 30 inches, which can be cut into six 11 x 10 inch pieces. After this paper gets wet, your project will curl. Simply wait for the piece to dry, then press it under a stack of books or other heavy, flat surface.

ILLUSTRATION BOARD

This product works very well, for several reasons. The paper consists of many layers and is offered in several different types.

One type of **CRESCENT ILLUSTRATION BOARD** that produces great results is the 310 Cold Press. This is a good place to start. If you decide to pursue this hobby, at some point you may wish to explore the illustration board that is made with the Hot Press method. Some of the photos in this book show works which used the 215 Hot Press Illustration board.

SCOPE AND SIZE

As you gain skills and confidence, you may want to try working with larger sizes. Starting out, you may choose to practice with smaller size pictures.

You may find it advantageous to cut the board into either 10 x 10 inch squares or a similar size depending upon the material. A 20 x 30 inch piece of illustration board can be cut into 6 pieces for example.

Use scissors to cut tissue paper into quarter size sheets. Cut just one sheet at a time as needed, and keep the rest of the sheets the full size.

You can cut illustration board with scissors if you do not have access to a **heavy-duty paper trimmer.** Though not required, a trimmer is handy for cutting illustration board or poster board into smaller pieces.

SAMPLE ORDER FOR MATERIALS

SMALL ORDER: This would be an appropriate order for an individual artist who wanted to explore the hobby without buying too many supplies.

Quantity: (2) Crescent illustration board – 310 Cold Press. Size 20 x 30 inch sheet. (Purchase a smaller size if you do not have a paper trimmer.)

Quantity: (1) Tissue Paper – Spectra 24 Sheet Assortment.

With these supplies, you can make 12 small paintings. Please also review the Tools and Workspace chapter to determine if you will need any additional supplies.

LARGE ORDER: For more than one artist, or an artist working on multiple projects, order the same supplies from Order One, then order:

Illustration board as needed. Crescent 310 Cold Press. Also, try the Strathmore Bristol Board or the Crescent Hot Press 215 Board if your budget permits.

Spectra Art Tissue. Consider ordering one additional variety pack. Then, consider ordering individual colors of Spectra Art Tissue.

Canary Yellow, Orchid, and Blush Pink. These three colors work well when used in the foreground of a landscape and combine with other colors easily.

Azure Blue and Sky Blue are great for making skies and water scenes.

TOOLS AND WORKSPACE

A utility paint **brush** (2"). An inexpensive, household paint brush is to wet the board and wet the paper

A smaller paint brush (artist brush with a small tip) may be useful for gaining control over small pieces of tissue paper such as a tree or animal.

One or more **plastic cups** or containers for water.

A level **work surface** that can handle the water and colored ink. The table should be covered or protected from the ink and water. Exercise steps to protect furniture and the floor from any ink spills. I sometimes cover my work table with the plastic from a flat, unopened trash bag.

Having a sheet of stiff **cardboard** or plastic to place under the project will allow you to tilt the wet board if necessary. Controlling which direction the ink moves can be very helpful.

Regular scissors can be used to cut tissue paper and poster board into smaller sizes. Regular scissors are great for cutting simple shapes, like a mountain.

For fine detail work (especially trees or animals) use **small scissors** and a **stapler** for holding multiple sheets in place while cutting. (Part II)

A **trash container** is used to place discarded and wet tissue paper.

OPTIONAL TOOLS

Protective Clothing or Latex Gloves. Wet tissue paper may stain objects which it comes in contact with. Either wait for projects to completely dry, or consider using latex gloves. Otherwise, warm water and bar soap will be needed to remove any ink from hands and fingers.

USING THE BRUSH

When working with illustration board, have your tissue paper already torn or cut to the desired size.

For most of the projects, I used scissors to cut the full 20 x 30 inch sheet of tissue paper into four quarters.

Begin by wetting the illustration or poster board using a paintbrush and clean water. Taking this extra step will go a long way toward getting good color coverage.

With the illustration board lightly coated with water, place the tissue paper onto the board. Use a very small amount of water and brush over the tissue paper and edges, until the paper is covered. Then wait for the project to dry.

In this demonstration, I have kept the tissue paper somewhat flat. But there will still likely be some lines and creases.

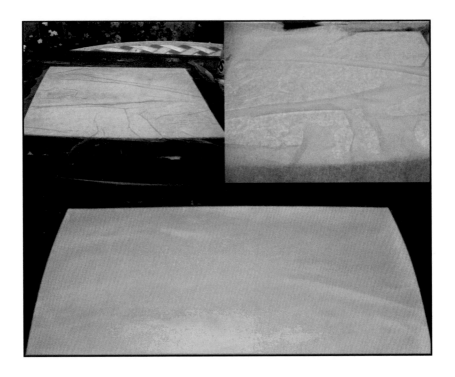

The upper right corner image shows ridges and creases that will need to be smoothed over with the wet brush. The lower photograph shows the illustration board dry.

Try to use just enough water to get good coverage. Then use the damp or dry brush to gently smooth out any air bubbles.

As you use the paint brush to apply water on tissue paper, the paper should never tear. If the tissue paper tears, you will need to consider a different brush or a gentler application.

START WET

For some types of illustration and poster board, wetting the surface of the paper before placing the tissue paper on the illustration board, is going to make a huge difference in how well the ink is transferred.

To illustrate this point, the illustration board on the left was painted wet with water, while the illustration board on the right was kept dry. Then, the tissue paper was added and gently painted wet with water. While wet, both pieces looked the same. But notice the difference when the project dried and the paper was removed.

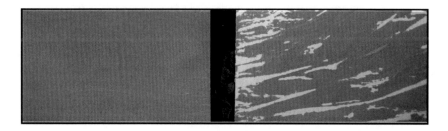

With practice, you may be able to skip this step, and start with a dry board. Otherwise, wet the surface of the poster or illustration board first, to gain maximum color distribution, and minimize any white space.

TEXTURE

There are occasions when you may choose to keep the tissue paper smooth and flat, and other times when you want to add some texture before you wet the paper with water. Often, the extra lines and creases will add points of interest.

This illustration shows a slightly crumpled piece of tissue paper on a wet board. You can also smooth over some of the creases and folds in the paper using the wet brush.

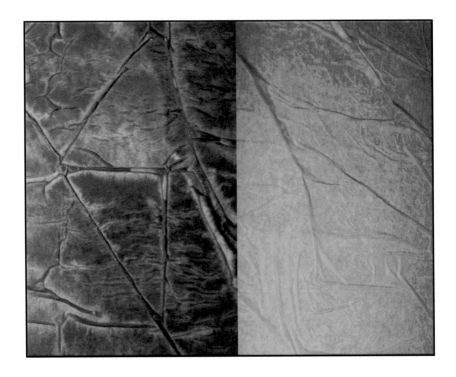

When you desire an even application of ink, keep the tissue paper as flat as possible. For example, if you plan to create a base color, you may find it advantageous to keep the paper somewhat smooth and free from wrinkles.

THE GRAIN

Paper is identified as either grain short or grain long. The grain refers to the strands and fibers that are used to create the paper. The fibers in the paper tend to align in one direction or the other.

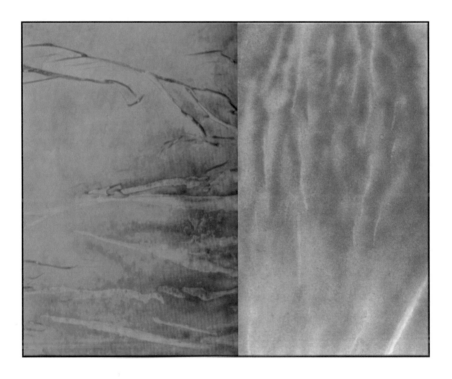

Tissue paper has a grain. The grain is parallel to either the short side or the long side depending on how the paper is cut.

Spectra tissue paper is grain long. The grain on the tissue paper runs with the long side of the paper. If you gently tear the tissue paper in the same direction as the grain, you will find it tears easily. Tearing against the grain, the tear may be more jagged.

PROJECT 1: MAGIC FOREST

Use Crescent Board, Strathmore Bristol Board, or Poster Board. The photographs show **Crescent Cold Press 310** Illustration Board.

Tissue Paper: **Seal Brown** for the tree trunks.
Goldenrod or color of your choice for the background. To make the green shown in the photo, use Goldenrod first, then **French Blue**.

Gather materials first and cut the brown tissue paper into six to ten narrow strips of varied width. Taper the strips smaller on one end.

If you are using the yellow practice board, wet the board with water, then skip ahead and position the trees. Otherwise, wet the board with water and cover with Goldenrod. Or, for the green background, start with French Blue.

Paint wet with water. After a minute, carefully remove and discard the tissue paper.

Position the tree trunks randomly on the damp board. While holding in place, gently use the paint brush to paint over the tree trunks with water. Use broad strokes with the big brush. Some brown ink may begin to bleed.

Cover the tree trunks with Goldenrod, with the grain oriented horizontally. Paint wet using minimal water. Avoid going back and forth too much. Then, most importantly, allow the project to dry.

PRETREATING THE BOARD

In some instances, the most important thing you can do when you begin a project, is to eliminate the white space wherever white is not used in the picture. Taking this extra step, will elevate the quality of your work.

For some projects, you may wish to cover the entire surface with a single color. On other occasions, it may be helpful to use different colors for specific regions of the picture. This is a great use for any scrap pieces.

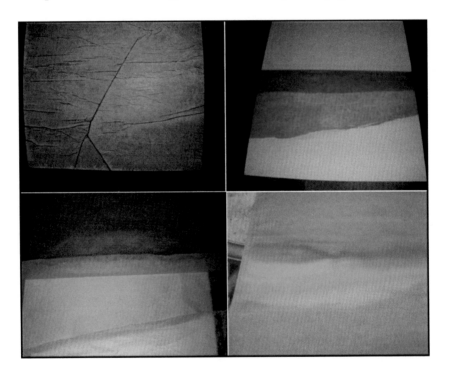

After pretreating the board, it will be up to you to decide when to proceed with the next phase. Depending upon the material, it may be beneficial to allow the board to completely dry before continuing. When in doubt, dry it out!

OVERLAPPING

When you overlap tissue paper, you can expect all kinds of wonderful things to happen. This is where the magic begins.

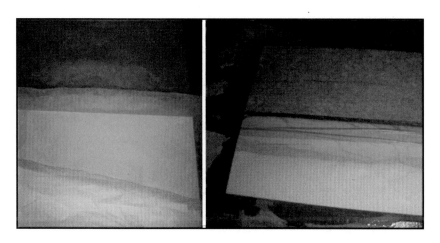

Notice where the blue and yellow overlap, you can expect to see some green. Where the pink and blue overlap, you will find a beautiful purple.

At times, you may be surprised by how the different colors interact.

Depending on the materials you are working with, placing a sheet of red tissue paper over a piece of blue tissue paper may be quite different than placing the blue tissue paper on top of the red.

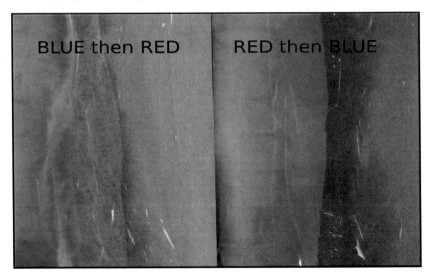

ADDING COLORS

One easy method to add color to an existing piece of tissue paper, is to tear a strip of paper that you can hold one end in one hand while using the wet paint brush in the other hand to tap out some ink.

With Canary Yellow tissue paper on the board, one small piece of red is plenty to make a beautiful orange color for the sky.

As you wet the strip, drag it across the tissue paper quickly. Then use the brush and additional water if necessary to achieve the desired color.

Allow the project to dry before continuing.

This technique works best when applying a dark color on top of a lighter color.

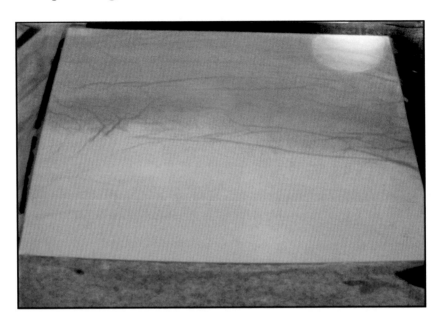

You can also use this method to transfer ink from tissue paper directly onto the surface of the illustration board. Work quickly to avoid creating an unintended shape. Then, cover the ink with tissue paper.

PROJECT 2: MAGIC MOUNTAIN

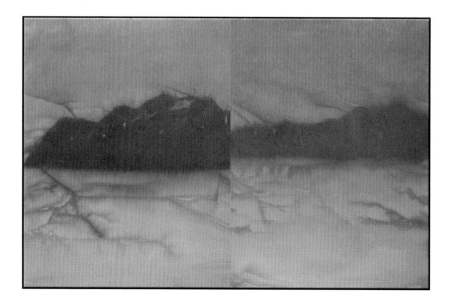

Material Used – Crescent Illustration Board (left side) or Strathmore Bristol Board (right side). The photograph reflects the blur in the finished piece.

Colors Used – Canary Yellow, Seal Brown and National Green. Red and orange ink added to sky.

Use scissors to cut the mountain shape before beginning. Make the mountain two sheets thick by folding a piece of Seal Brown Tissue paper in half.

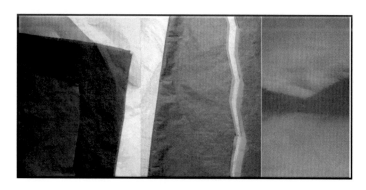

With the paper oriented in the **cross grain** direction, cut a jagged line a couple inches away from the edge of the paper. At this point, keep the tissue paper flat.

Then trim away beneath to create the shape of the mountain.

Paint the illustration board wet with water. Cover the entire board with Canary Yellow and paint wet with water. Wait a minute, then remove and discard sheet of yellow tissue paper.

Before placing the mountain on the wet board, add some crumple to the paper. Then place the mountain onto the wet paper. Gently paint wet with water and keep the project level. Notice the direction of the brush. In this case, I am tapping the water from the brush onto the brown mountain.

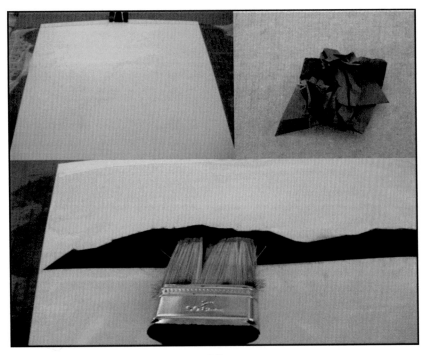

You may see some of the brown ink migrating above and below.

Next, add the strip of National Green along the bottom portion of the brown mountain. Put the green right on top of the brown. Wet it with water. Green ink will start seeping out.

Quickly cover the project with a sheet of yellow tissue paper, and wet with minimal water. Paint the entire illustration board wet with water, including the sky and the mountain. Try not to over brush.

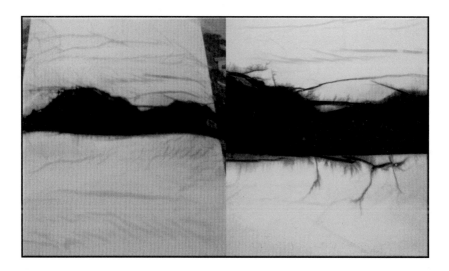

If you wish, use the strip of red tissue paper to add color to the sky. This additional water used to paint in the sky will also help push the brown ink from the mountain downward.

By hand, or by prop, gently tilt the project slightly so that the ink flows from the mountain toward the bottom.

Be careful not to tilt for more than a few seconds. Often, after you return the project to a level state, the flow of ink will continue for several minutes.

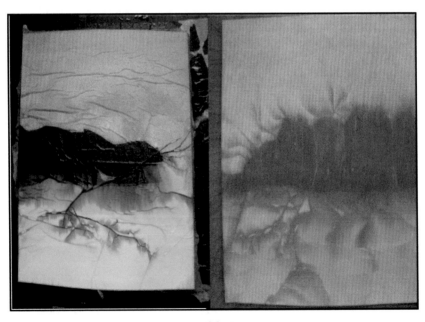

COMBINING SHEETS

You can make spectacular effects when you combine two colors.

You can make an award winning sky using just two sheets of tissue paper. This is so easy, and yet so beautiful!

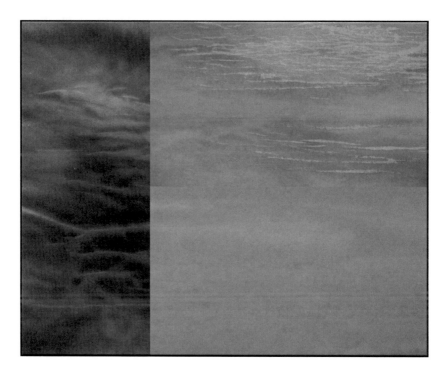

Watch the magic happen when the beautiful blue and pink combine to make this unique and stunning sky!

This will work with many combinations. I recommend starting by combining one of the lighter shades of blue (Sky, French or Azure) with a pink or light purple.

With one sheet of tissue paper already wet with water, try adding a different color on top.

In the example below, a darker shade of blue on top of the lighter shade will distinguish the sky from the water area.

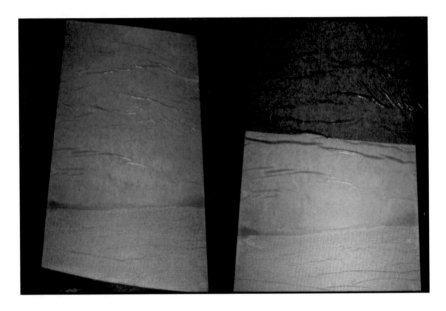

This will work well with all kinds of color combinations. Put the light colors down first and darker colors on top.

In some cases, the color and ink from a third sheet may bleed through. But most of the time, two sheets is sufficient.

Lastly, to transfer the beautiful details, you want the ink to be as close to the illustration board as possible.

PROJECT 3: MAGIC SKY

To make the sky, use **French Blue** and **Blush Pink.**
Use Crescent Illustration Board, Bristol Board or poster
board.

In my example, I have used the entire illustration board.
You decide where you want your beautiful sky.

1. Paint the surface wet with water.

2. Cover the sky area with the Blush Pink tissue
   paper and paint wet with water.

3. **Leave the pink tissue paper** on and cover the
   sky area with medium blue tissue paper and paint
   wet with water.

Congratulations! When this project is dry, you will have a beautiful and inspirational sky.

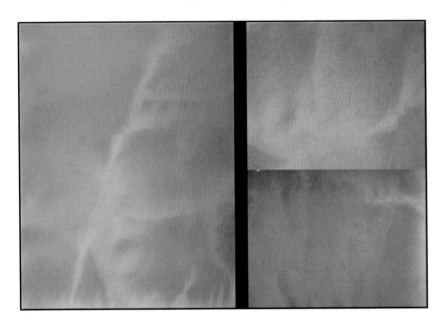

You can also achieve great results with Crescent Illustration board and Strathmore Bristol Board.

SHAPES AND OBJECTS

One easy method to add shapes and objects is to create a pattern and cut the tissue paper using a pattern.

Draw or trace a pattern on a piece of scratch paper. Or find a silhouette image on the internet and print from a computer.

Once you have your pattern available, choose the color tissue paper. In the time it takes to cut one tree, you can cut 16 or more trees, so you may want to vary your colors.

Folding the tissue paper will make it firmer, and easier to cut and will give you many trees from a single cut. For example, fold the tissue four times to yield 16 trees.

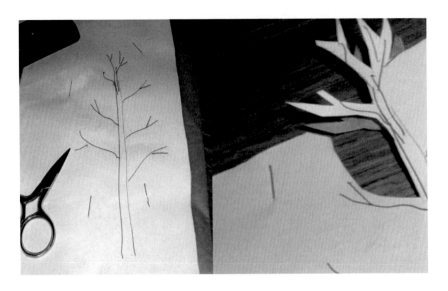

Use staples to hold the pattern in place over the folded tissue paper.

You may find it easier to start cutting the areas with any fine details. Save the more solid sections for later. Add staples as you cut to keep things together.

SHAPES AND OBJECTS (WET)

Objects, such as trees and animals can be added to your pictures at any time. However, if you already have a dark background, it may be challenging to add a tree.

<u>One method is to add the tree or other objects before creating the background</u>. This method is easier and may be better suited for younger artists.

The coyote was cut from black tissue paper and the tree was cut from the Seal Brown tissue paper. I positioned the tree first, then covered the wet tree with tissue paper.

When a piece of brown or black tissue paper is placed on a wet board, the ink is going to flow. You can use your wet brush to gently push some of the ink away from the tree. When using black tissue paper, you may want to use a generous amount of water because of all the ink that will disburse.

Position and hold in place until you have gently painted the object or shape with water.

Allow the ink to flow and disburse across the surface of the board. Then cover with one or more sheets of tissue paper. Brush with water again to help disburse the ink from the object. Notice the black "shadows" around the coyote.

Above. Objects with more detail can be more challenging. To wet the surface, try painting the branches gently from the trunk toward the edges, to help keep the tree in place.

SHAPES AND OBJECTS (DRY)

With this method, object such as trees and animals are added after the background is established.

This method can be used to produce stunning results, however more patience and attention to detail is required.

While you do not need to "paint" the object in great detail, you do need to work with a small wet brush, making contact with only the object.

Please also see the information on "Extracting Ink" which follows, as it is especially relevant and helpful. You may prefer to "paint" the object with ink.

STEPS TO ADD OBJECTS

Prepare your background so that you can work on a dry surface.

Cut the object from a pattern. Review the information in the Chapter "Extracting Ink". Then extract a small amount of ink in a plastic cup.

With the object positioned in place, wet the small paintbrush with ink and tap off any excess before using the brush. Position the object and hold in place as you carefully dab the object and allow the ink to spread.

To cover the little duck with ink, I used a small artist brush and dabbed the duck with the brush just four times. To create an amazing shade of brown, use this **magic formula** – Cut the shape from Goldenrod Tissue Paper and paint it with the ink from Azure Blue.

DIFFUSION

Diffusion is defined as: The intermingling of substances by the natural movement of their particles. (Source: Meriam Webster)

The texture and grain of the tissue paper can be used to create the appearance of trees and branches. This technique can be used by itself to make or to add detail to an existing picture.

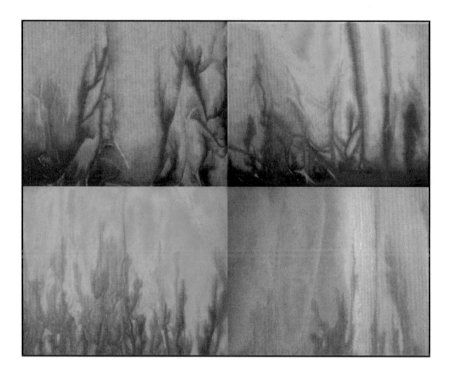

For small, closely entwined trees, be sure to crumple the tissue paper tightly. If you want the trees to be longer and less gnarly, crumple the paper less.

You can also smooth out the upper portion with a clean brush to keep the ink away.

The direction of the grain is important. The creases, folds and lines in the tissue paper will direct and influence the ink.

Tilting the board will increase or decrease the flow of ink.

Like magic, the little grasses and weeds create a beautiful meadow.

PROJECT 4: MAGIC MEADOW

Use Crescent Board, Strathmore Bristol Board, or poster board. The photographs show **Crescent Cold Press 310** Illustration Board.

Tissue Paper: **Canary Yellow** or color of your choice for the background. A small piece of black is used to make the picture shown in the photograph.

Having **a piece of cardboard underneath** the project will allow you to easily tilt the project for a few seconds. Or, insert a pencil or other object underneath to control the direction of the ink flow.

Begin by wetting the board with water, cover with yellow tissue paper, and wet again with water.

Allow at least some drying before removing the yellow tissue paper, and cover with a fresh piece of Canary Yellow with the grain of the paper oriented vertically.

Wet the surface with water and use the brush to smooth out the upper portion. This will help keep the ink in the lower portion of the picture.

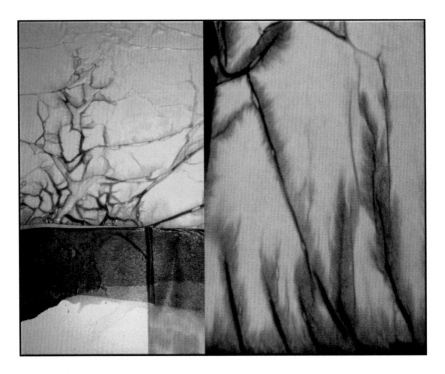

Add a small piece of tissue paper along the bottom edge of the illustration board. Black works great. Here, I am using a dark blue. Then wet the tissue paper to release the ink. Remember to clean the brush before using elsewhere on the picture.

If after 30 seconds, the black ink has not moved onto the yellow tissue paper, add a minimal amount of water. Tilt or slip a small object under the edge of the poster board and let gravity go to work.

The process of the ink moving along the creases may take 15 minutes, which is why you want to control the amount of water you apply. Once the ink starts moving, it will continue to move for several minutes.

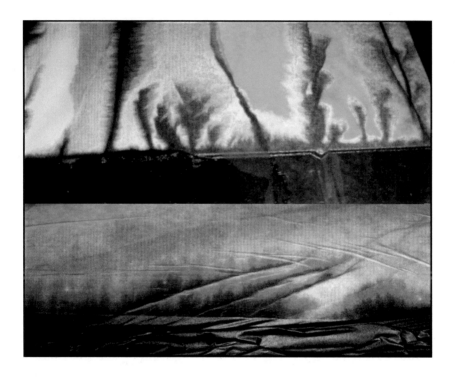

Notice how the beautiful red shadow is released from the black tissue paper. More magic!

EXTRACT THE INK

Extracting the ink from the tissue paper will give you more infinite possibilities and more magic! By mixing, you can achieve custom colors.

This works best with dark colors like brown, black, violet, dark blue, dark green, and dark red. There is no ink to extract from white.

Use a ¼ sheet of tissue paper, either folded or crumpled into a small wad and a plastic cup with ¼ cup of water.

Stir a few times with a small paintbrush or other object and wait a minute or two for the ink to completely release.

There are several advantages to having the ink ready in this format. Just think about the possibilities!

You can use the colored water to paint and pretreat the boards. You can use the colored water to target specific sections. By mixing ink, you can create custom colors!

Ink on a dry brush used to make some blades of grass.

I used a blue and gray ink to paint the mountain.

WORKING IN STAGES

On some occasions, the perfect picture can be made in a single session. Maybe the piece only needed a couple of colors.

On other occasions, you may decide you want to work in stages. For example, it might be more convenient to make the sky today, and the beautiful mountains tomorrow.

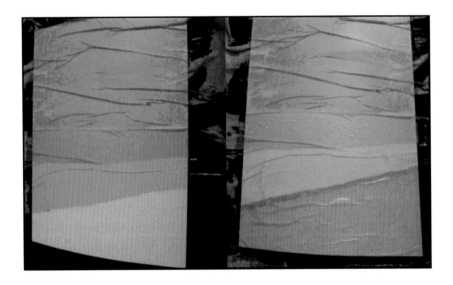

Whether you choose Bristol Board, Crescent Illustration Board, or some poster board at your local store, the surface of the paper will determine how well the colors and details transfer.

Some materials will work well when they get wet once and are allowed to dry. The same material (poster board for example) may not do well if you then try to revisit the project to make additions or changes. The second time the product gets wet, may limit the amount of detail that you can achieve.

If you plan to work on a project in stages, it is important to choose a material that will hold up under the repeated exposure to water.

In the piece shown below, I let the mountain dry overnight. The next day, I worked on the foreground.

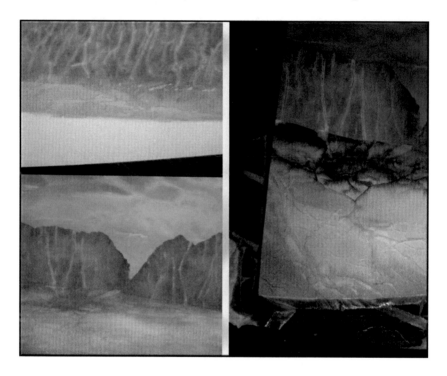

My experience is that the **Crescent 310 Cold Press** Illustration board holds up well through this process, even though it is a thin board.

WATER

With so many shades of blue available, water is easy to include in your projects.

Folding the edge down on the blue tissue paper will give you a straight line for the horizon and can help keep the ink from moving into other areas of the picture.

Keeping the water area covered while you work on the rest of the project may help you maintain control of the shore line.

Sky Blue, French Blue and Azure Blue are all good choices for making water scenes.

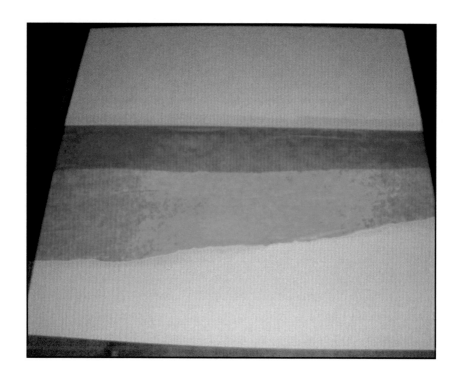

If you start with a light blue color on the board, you can add darker shades of blue by extracting ink.

MOUNTAINS

When I make mountains, I like to orient the tissue paper in the vertical position. Sometimes I use scissors to cut the mountain shape. If you tear the shape by hand, take your time, especially if you are be tearing against the grain.

Instead of painting with water, try using the ink. Be sure to allow the tissue paper to dry to capture some of the beautiful depth and detail.

The photograph shows the wet image (left) and the finished picture (right). Crescent Illustration Board.

Folding the bottom edge of the mountain will help prevent ink from flowing into other parts of the picture.

Overlap the mountain with another piece of tissue paper if you want the ink to flow down from the mountain.

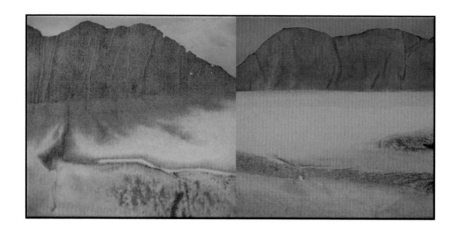

The photograph (left) shows Seal Brown overlapping Sky Blue. Spring Green folded next to Sky Blue (Right)

The overlapping tissue paper allows the ink to diffuse into the ridges and creases. Notice below, how the overlapping tissue paper provides a path for the ink to flow.

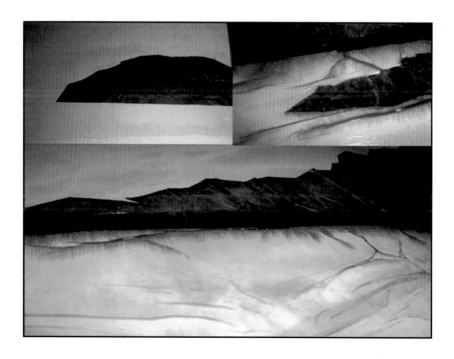

FOREGROUNDS

When working with the foreground, you may find it more efficient to work with the light colors first. You can easily make something darker.

Canary Yellow, Orchid and Pink all work well together.

After establishing the water and sky areas, use any of those colors to start the base. You can always start with yellow and replace or add pieces of pink and orchid. Use yellow along the edges of the water if you want to add up some green.

You may decide to keep the blue tissue paper for the water area in place until the project is finished. This usually helps define the shoreline.

ADD POINTS OF INTEREST

This is an easy way to add ink and some points of interest to a specific part of the picture. Twist or **roll a strip of Seal Brown tissue paper** tightly to resemble a small piece of string.

Position the string where you want to create some plant life. Wet the string in select places to release the ink. Remove or leave in place.

This effect also works well on watercolor paper, shown on the right side of the photo below.

Use a small strand or string of twisted tissue paper, or add some ink directly using a small brush.

The image below (right) shows a custom color ink. Through evaporation, the ink had become rather thick, and produced a beautiful effect.

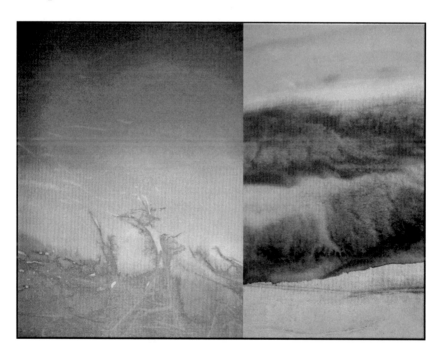

STRATEGIES FOR SUCCESS

CONTROL THE WATER

With bleeding art tissue, it is important to control the amount of water that you use. Too much water is going to cause warping or bubbling of the illustration board, or may cause some of the layers to peel or separate.

If warping occurs, it usually begins on the edges of your project. Some warping may be unavoidable or it may be a sign that you are using too much water. Stop work and allow some drying.

For some of your projects, you will want to apply multiple colors. You may need to **allow some drying between steps** to help prevent any warping, curling, or separation of the paper.

You may find much less warping occurs if you simply rotate the illustration or poster board before applying any water. Remember the paper you are working on has a grain, just like the tissue paper.

You can also **press the work** under a stack of books or other flat, heavy object for several hours, or overnight.

LET THE PROJECT DRY

The illustration below shows the how the ink flowed from the black tissue paper along the edges, over a period of about fifteen minutes. Then, I needed to wait additional time.

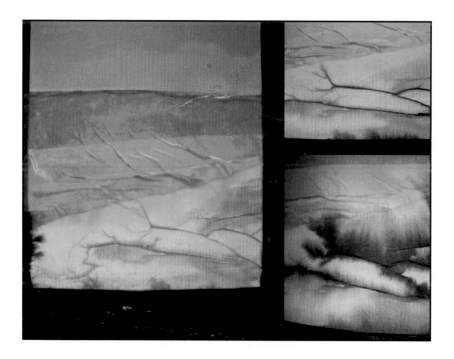

If you remove the tissue paper too soon, you risk losing some of the detail and interesting colorations. Wait at least an hour. The surface may still be damp, but the colors should be in place.

SIZE THE PROJECT

Many times, the most interesting part of a painting will be found in a selected region of the work. Working with larger pieces of illustration board, has many advantages.

Using a larger board will allow you to choose the best and most interesting part of the picture as well as trim off any unwanted edges.

AVOID EXCESSIVE BRUSH STROKES

The tissue paper blends the beautiful colors. Let the magic happen. **Too many brush strokes** may diminish the beautiful veins and creases that exist in the tissue paper.

The veins in the tissue paper will transfer to the illustration board. The veins will also influence the flow of ink that you introduce from other sources.

DISCOVER COLOR COMBINATIONS

Black and Yellow – Inserting the Yellow Under the Black creates a rich landscape.

Two Sheets of Orchid, Small Amount of Black creates a Marble Effect.

Use Goldenrod Tissue Paper with Black or dark ink to make an amazing shade of brown.

The photograph below shows a picture made with just pink, blue, and black. (Made on the Strathmore Bristol Paper)

Notice the magic gray color where the Azure Blue overlapped the black tissue paper. A similar effect can be achieved with Azure Blue and Violet.

LEARN FROM EVERY PIECE

Even if a project does not go as planned, look for an opportunity to learn. For example, you might discover that when working with green, too much green was used. Just a dab would have done.

Or, within the project, you may be able to find one part that went well. Or you may discover a new combination of colors that will inspire you to try again.

THANK YOU!

Thank you for sharing your time with me. I hope you enjoy this fascinating art form.

Derek Phoenix

Made in the USA
Lexington, KY
19 April 2019